VIS TO HEAVEN

BY
REV'D DAVID PETERSON

PUBLISHED BY
KRATOS PUBLISHERS

VISITS TO HEAVEN

Copyright ©2022 by REVEREND DAVID PETERSON

ISBN: 9798844292545

PUBLISHED BY

TABLE OF CONTENT

Visit 1 --- 5

Visit 2 --- 6

Visit 3 --- 7

Visit 4 --- 8

Visit 5 --- 9

Visit 6 --- 10

Visit 7 --- 11

Visit 8 --- 12

Visit 9 --- 13

Visit 10 -- 14

Visit 11 -- 15

Visit 12 -- 16

Visit 13 -- 17

Visit 14 -- 18

Visit 15 -- 19

Visit 16 -- 20

Visit 17 -- 21

Visit 18 -- 22

Visit 19 -- 23

Visit 20 -- 24

Visit 21 -- 25

Visit 22 -- 26

Visit 23 -- 27

Visit 24 -- 28

Visit 25 -- 29

Visit 26 -- 30

Visit 27 -- 31

Visit 28 -- 32

Visit 29 -- 33

Visit 30 -- 34

Visit 31 -- 35

Visit 32 -- 36

Visit 33 -- 37

Visit 34 -- 38

Visit 35 -- 39

Visit 36 -- 40

Visit 37 -- 41

Visit 38 -- 42

Visit 39 -- 43

Visit 40 -- 44

VISIT 1

The very first time I had a vision of heaven, I was in a prayer meeting with my older sister. When I closed my eyes, I saw the beautiful Kingdom of Heaven and people just casually walking around engaging in conversation with one another. The main emotion I felt in the air as if it was like how oxygen is on the earth was love. I saw Jesus and He was black with an afro. I asked him where God is as I thought his presence was the hype I experience at church but it wasn't, it was pure love. The atmosphere was filled with love in the purest and most simple form. It wasn't complicated at all. It was the pure love you had for friends, family and pets.

When I asked Jesus where God was, He simply laughed and walked off in a way as if He was happy, I was there. An angel said that they would give me a tour. So, the angel took me to a library and took down a book with my name on it. Some pages was written and some was blank. I asked "why are some pages blank?" and the angel said "everything you say, do and think we write it down. But when you repent all your sin are erased from your book."

VISIT 2

I was in Heaven and the Lord assigned an angel to me called Samson to show me around. I asked if he was the Samson from the bible and he said no. The Angel took me to a library and showed me the last thing written about me which was 'David did his grime set for the Lord and fell more and more in love with God.' Then Samson took me to the 'Grace Hills' where angels pick dandelions and blow them onto the earth and grace would fall on mankind, specifically on the humble and prisoners who had repented. I then met the Lord in His chambers for a debrief before I came back into my body.

VISIT 3

I went to heaven and saw God the Father. It was as if the Sun was the form of His face. So much light, glory and majesty. He is the light of the universe. There was a party for me when I arrived, I asked God why? He said because I had chosen him. I went to a swimming pool and a whale jumped out, someone asked if I wanted to go for a ride. It felt as if I didn't have a choice, I made a slight split decision to say yes and I was on the whale. As I was on the whale it dived back into the pool and through the wall of the swimming pool and down a valley I was then inside the whale and was able to control it. I then went to the earth for a bit and saw my body sitting in the loft.

I then went to a war where Jesus was leading an army. He was like superman slash Dr Strange. Christians would die and respawn in heaven and re-join the war. The demons we were fighting had cat/crab bodies and spiders for heads. One thousand years went by after we had won the war then the devil snuck back into the peaceful loving world. Before being defeated forever as people hadn't respawned for ages. God said the mark of the beast is an open choice to serve him. It's CHOICE. Once you make the wrong choice in the last days to serve the anti-Christ for eternity, you are marked.

VISIT 4

I was in heaven and everyone cheered my arrival and there was like a werewolf bat looking creature brought before me. God then removed a werewolf spirit from within me. It apologised to God for trying to make me a part of their dynasty. God then filled me with music instead and said there will come a time when I will make great music for God.

VISIT 5

I was taken into heaven and I saw a light house and when Christians would sin in a big way or backslide, I would see a lighthouse crumble that would need to be rebuilt if the person humbly turned to God fully. Then I saw celebrities, they were called 'big nets' in heaven. They were like moving giants being worked on to be saved. I saw Kylie Mange, Will and Jaden, Daft punk, Jedwad and the people who played Kid and play from house party.

VISIT 6

I went to Heaven. I was talking to God the Father and I was in the form of a green seed. Then an angel took me to a room where you can choose a book in the bible to re-live and the stories of people in Heaven you can also re-live. You take the book from the library place it onto like a white letter box looking door and the story of that person plays and you can re-live it like a virtual cinema but you can't change what happens. Then I went to the flying room where you go in to just fly to endless heights and lengths and depths but you always know your way back. Then I was consumed with the fire of the Holy Spirit and came back to my body.

VISIT 7

I was taken up into Heaven by a cloud of His Glory. I looked at God's throne and it was empty, then God was standing behind me. He turned into a black cat with white patches and ran off. I chased after him. He then turned into a man and was showing me how to cook. Then the Holy Spirit came in the form of a dove and in an instant I was back in my body.

VISIT 8

I was in heaven, an angel took me to a room of mirrors. As you look into the mirrors you can re-live the lives of everyone on your mother's side of the family. This was not virtual reality this was real. Then I was taken to the highest Heaven called the 7th Heaven. I was in the mind of God and I could see that at the fore front of God's mind was the wedding feast between Jesus and the church. It was a room with a huge see-through golden brain in it. The room was like a command centre. You could see the electric neurons moving across the brain.

As I looked through the window of the command centre and I saw a beautiful valley. I noticed that there was no sun shining, just a radiant light from God light up the whole of heaven, his Glory is all the light needed. I was taken to the heart of God. It saw a large diamond filled with love. Many people were in God's heart especially sinners that would eventually repent.

VISIT 9

I was in Heaven and I saw a brown ugly creature being reprimanded. It was the devil telling God the sins of a well-known preachers and that of all the saints. Then he looked at me and said 'what is he doing here? He is refusing to breakthrough to the higher level.' Then he tried to attack me but the angels restrained him. I was also given power over him and I kicked him out of Heaven. I was then taken to a mountain in Heaven and God showed me how much he loved me on a screen showing all the things he did for me. Then he looked at me and said that he wished all believed.

VISIT 10

I was taken to Heaven and I was lifted onto people's shoulders. They were singing songs about me. In a moment, I was placed before the throne of God and Jesus himself took me on a tour. He said He was excited to see me. I thought why? I'm a nobody. He showed me bread in Heaven that was continually being broken for the crumbs to fall down from heaven like mini sermons for preachers to preach and people in churches to receive to get them through the day. Then I saw a room where people's shadow was turning into shadows of light, once they received the revelation of the Old Testament being a shadow of the new. Jesus took me to the hall of faith in Heaven and said fame is not a bad thing as long as you're not worshiping it.

Almost all of Heaven was in the hall of faith except those who came after the great tribulation. In the last room crosses were being made and sent to believers, those that accepted them went to heaven and those that didn't went to hell. As you need a cross to give in exchange for a crown. Jesus and I then had a private conversation which I can not share in this book. As He was taking me on this tour, His ethnicity kept changing. He was a white crusader, an Asian old man, an Indian man, a Jamaican with locks and an African villager king!

VISIT 11

I went to Heaven and I was surrounded by mirrors then I saw Morpheus from the matrix and I became Neo and loads of guns appeared. It was symbolic of being equipped to fight the devil and his evil. Then there were loads of people in the same situation as if we were like Christ was on the Earth. Every believer was like a mini-Neo. As we know Jesus is the 'One' but as we bare his Spirit, we share in this responsibility to rage war against the evil one and fight for Heaven.

VISIT 12

I went to Heaven, it was as if I burst through the ground this time. I was dressed as Neo from the matrix with a long black jacket. I was in the throne room of God and as I approached, God's angels held me down. Then a rainbow from God hit me in my chest. God then asked me to look at Him and all I saw was light. I began to see moments of my life. I saw a time my father came into my room to check on me when I was asleep. God would come in after him to also check on me. So, I was being checked on twice in the night.

Then God showed me how to release His Spirit and said that He showed me before but I allowed a demon to get in the way. So, this time I should treat it like fasting, in that once I commit to a fast, I shouldn't break it. Unless the Lord tells me to. God also told me that if I keep my heart filled with love that His Spirit will follow like in the book of Acts. I was told that I must keep my heart open to pain so that God can mature me and Christ will be shown to me through the fellowship of suffering.

VISIT 13

I appeared in Heaven as a cherubim worshipping and God said I'll have a mansion in Heaven but He wants me to be one of His right hand men, constantly in the throne room worshipping him. This is my eternal desire. I said yes!

VISIT 14

I was in heaven and the Lord showed me a storm to hit London and said as a storm is hitting physically there will be one hitting spiritually to ripen the land for revival.

VISIT 15

I went to heaven before God and I was blasted by a bright light and the same ray of light was love. The love of God. I felt it then I began to see the time in my life when I broke my arm and split my head open and almost die. God was there at those moments catching me, protecting me and making sure I didn't die.

VISIT 16

I was in Heaven and I saw someone dressed as trunks from Dragon ball Z minus the sword. But his face was a white flame. I asked who he was, as he put me on his back and started flying with me. He said He is the Holy Spirit. He said He wanted to show me something and took me to a room filed with boxes and in the boxes were people's prayer requests and there was a corner in the room that led to earth and I had more than one box in there from different times in my life that I was close to God.

The Holy Spirit opened a box and prayer requests started pouring them out. They poured out onto the earth into my life. One was so big it got stuck. The Holy Spirit said some requests will only be released when you get to Heaven and some only God can release. Not angels. The Holy Spirit caused the prayer request that was too big to fit through the tunnel to appear and travel into my life. It was the prayer request to have money flowing like tap water.

VISIT 17

I was in Heaven sitting at a table and there were different people being inducted as a Chaplain in Heaven and I was one of them. So, there was a massive feast and celebration.

VISIT 18

I was in Heaven and I saw the whole of Heaven was watching the death of Jesus when it took place. There were cracks in Heaven's walls as the Father's heart was releasing tremors because He wanted to be reconciled with man his love for man not being fulfilled could have destroyed everything. So, the day Jesus died, the walls of Heaven were red covered in His blood. Heaven was red that day. When he rose again from the dead and the tomb opened, a burst of light hit Heaven and the cracks in the walls mended and Heaven was brighter and the red had disappeared.

VISIT 19

I was in Heaven and there was a war. I saw the statue head of the eagle of the four living creatures falling apart. Then I saw the devil release dark matter to blind God for five split seconds which was enough to wreak havoc. Then God revealed a side of him that the devil was unaware of. His name is Jesus. Jesus came out of God on a horse dressed as a king. He went right into the centre of the battle and lifted the devil off his feet. The devil then stabbed him with a half-moon shaped sword in his side, under his third rib.

They shot arrows in Christ's feet and hands. The fallen began to claw at his back and one who would later rule over the spirit of anger bite Jesus' head because they could see He was unstoppable! Jesus with one right hand punch sent the devil crashing to earth and peace became still once again.

VISIT 20

I went to Heaven, I was in the throne room of God. The Father was covered in Holy Ghost Fire and He handed me a baton. He said I will be one of His generals and spark 1-million-man revival in London. Many close to me and people who have never met me will be against me but I will hold God close to my heart.

VISIT 21

I went to heaven and was in the throne room of God and God took me to a room of pearls. The pearls were gifts and talents that God gave to the saints. Then He took me to a room of emeralds where if people were given the right names, it would help them get back home to Heaven through life and death.

VISIT 22

I went to heaven, I was in the throne room of God and I saw His back and cold air came out then I could see Joseph and Mary travelling and it was a cold night. Baby Jesus could have died but Mary kept his hands warm and warmed him up. Then I was back in the throne room and God said that I love him so much and always down play people because I believe God is amazing. But I'm afraid of my own pride but He is bigger than pride and He has made provisions for me that I am not an angel but a son of man.

VISIT 23

I had been listening to secular music the whole morning. So, I went to Heaven but this time I went in an elevator that took me to the gates. I saw millions of people being turned away. Some arguing that they should be in. Some trying to fight their way in but the angel at the gate had a list with your name, the date and time you are supposed to be there.

So, when I got to the gate, the angel said I can't come in because it's not my time but my name was on the list to enter Heaven. Then another angel came and said to let me in as I'm just visiting. So, I went in. There was a beautiful garden as you opened the gate then I asked why I didn't just go straight to the throne room. The angel said because I was listening to secular music all morning that it's not a sin but he would advise me to only watch Christian content.

VISIT 24

I was playing Gospel music and I went to Heaven and landed right on God's lap and we hugged each other and He said He loves me.

VISIT 25

I was in the throne room and angels arrested me and put me in a white cage and I couldn't return back to my body and they put a white bag over my head and took me to a tree in Nigeria. I saw a relative by a tree. They were performing demonic acts with a female spirit and God said that the 40-day water fast I was doing would break the curse. I then saw the spirit taking organs out of them and replacing them with black ones.

VISIT 26

I went to heaven and I had flowers and a red and pink box of chocolate that I gave to God. There were little red hearts moving from me to God and his heart got bigger and He said He will accept all forms of love from me as they will all manifest one day.

VISIT 27

I was in the throne room and I saw a golden scroll in God's hand and He said I'd die as a martyr on nation television. They will ask me to deny Christ and I'll say no and get shot in the head by a nine millimetre.

VISIT 28

I went to the throne room of God and He showed me the tree of life. The fruits were shiny silver and He told me to eat the fruit so I ate.

VISIT 29

I went to heaven, God showed me a worm hole looking thing that led straight to hell.

VISIT 30

I was in Heaven and I saw myself sitting on white stairs wearing a grey tracksuit reading how God had commanded the angels to write my book and I was getting upset as most of my life I was branded a villain. As the future me was thinking this, the worm hole to hell began to open. But the future me became grateful that he had made it and his clothes turned white and I became one with the future me. I saw my friend Ezekiel there Chris and Marylin, Paul, I saw my friend Joy who was going to hear Moses speak.

VISIT 31

I went to Heaven, I saw my dad and I was shocked he was there. He said my prayers and the blood of Jesus helped him. He asked me to bring Paul and Lois to the UK then God told him not to put that kind of pressure on me. I then saw a neighbour that had passed also in Heaven. He said I should be friends with one of his daughters. That if I remain friends with her that she won't go crazy and God agreed.

VISIT 32

I went to Heaven and there was a parade into my own country and there was a monument for me just at the entry gates of my country. To mark who the country belonged to.

VISIT 33

I was in the throne room and I gave The Father a huge hug and I said He has always been the love of my life.

VISIT 34

I went to Heaven and I had blood on my hands. Then I made a vow to God to never stop preaching the Gospel and trying my best to always be in a position to do full time ministry and to be a Man of God. I vowed to do this all the days of my life until I die no matter what happens or the scandals that may occur. Then my hands became as white as snow.

VISIT 35

I went to Heaven and I saw myself proposed to three women but it never worked out. Then God led me to the cross and I followed.

VISIT 36

I went to Heaven and I saw myself having a fight with lust, depression and suicide but I overcame by the blood of the lamb.

VISIT 37

I went to heaven and saw myself becoming so rich from being a prophet and I had no title but Reverend from the Church of England.

VISIT 38

I was in Heaven and I saw that I started my own ministry and I had branches all over the world and I was trying to take over the world for Jesus.

VISIT 39

I saw myself getting desperate for powers trying to use demons for power and asking the devil and he said God said that even if I ask him, God will not allow it because I belong to God. I'm God's property and He doesn't care how many times I get embarrassed on stage and I come to my right mind and cry with God's arms wrapped around me. This was symbolic to show that even when we sin or do bad things, as long as we repent and turn from our wicked ways God will always forgive us.

VISIT 40

I went to Heaven and I was in the throne room. God's heart grew and filled the whole of Heaven and God said "Tell my people that Heaven is a place of Love."

Printed in Great Britain
by Amazon

14506628R00031